Sarit Asherov

Stop Biting Your Nails!

Easily and with No Side Effects.

Sarit Asherov

Stop Biting Your Nails!

Easily and with No Side Effects.

Sarit Asherov
Stop Biting Your Nails!
Translation by: A.Q Translations
Proofreading: Ayala Gilboa

Cover and design: Lihi Lahav Studio
Illustrations: Yuval Bar-On

ISBN   978-965-7589-12-0
KIP- DISTRIBUTIONS

Table of Contents

Preface

I was introduced to the phenomenon of nail biting when I just started out in 2002, as a French manicurist. Among the compulsive nail biting clients I treated were women lawyers, psychologists, senior high-tech executives, mothers and even children (that's where it starts). They all expressed their desire to stop their nail biting - however none could. When women asked me if I also treat men, since their husband or son is a nail biter, I realized that nail biting is an addiction, similar to smoking. While nicotine is known to deteriorate the body and cause many health issues, nail biting is not accompanied by these health issues. However, in both cases, the habit is not incurable. I found a common denominator among nail biters and smokers, and as a former smoker, I understood that my experience could benefit my clients and anyone else interested in kicking the nail biting habit.

From my experience with nail biting men and women, I know that they bite due to anger, anxiety or any other restlessness they feel. I felt uncomfortable being around them (as a caregiver, and other clients felt the same), aesthetically and psychologically.

"I had a rough week," "I studied for a really big test and was under a lot of pressure," "My boss was driving me crazy," "I had a big fight with my husband," "I have no idea, I was watching a gripping movie on television and it just happened," "I just wanted to even it out..." - this is just a sample of the myriad of excuses I heard, and I call them that because the truth is that there is no good reason for nail biting. We would not do better on the test with damaged nails; our boss will not leave us in peace if we gnaw our fingernails raw, and neither will our husbands. The movie will not get more interesting with our hands in our mouths. These excuses remind me of my excuses for smoking. When I used to smoke, it was a cigarette for my nerves, a cigarette for boredom, a cigarette for focus, etc. I smoked until 2007, sometimes two packs a day. I was one of those people who say "I like smoking" and "I can quit anytime I want." I smoked every chance I had - even when it was inappropriate. I used to hide in some corner feeling like a criminal, smoke and spray some perfume or breathe spray so that people wouldn't notice. I smoked when I was "nervous" or "waiting" for something... I always believed that smoking was pushing me forward, helping me sell more products (I was a saleswoman), that "people would like me better," thus smoking took control of my life.

Looking at nail biters, one can find great resemblance to smokers. Both groups try to hide: We see them keeping their hands fisted, in their pockets or with their arms crossed. Nail biters are embarrassed by their habit and are reluctant to admit they have a problem. Smokers lie about extent, saying "I don't smoke; it's just two-three cigarettes a day." They do not understand that the number of cigarettes is irrelevant to the problem - one cigarette a day is enough to make someone a smoker. Nail biters are the same - they start with chewing on the skin around the nail, saying "I'm not biting the nail, I'm just evening out, clearing the skin," or "I've been biting my nails since I was a kid… it's genetic, you can't just stop."

Nail biting and smoking both involve an element of self-destruction. The sore around the nail, or the gravelly cough and chest pains, are an expression of our will to hurt and destroy ourselves, intentionally or subconsciously. The destruction lies deep within the biter's or smoker's subconscious.

In addition, it would be wrong to say that both cases are "intentional" - since the whole point here is creating a "think first" attitude and then realizing the source of the habit!!!

The purpose of this book is to help us go through the withdrawal process in stages, easily and gradually, with no side effects. When we quit a habit using willpower, but don't realize the meaning behind it, we could fall off the wagon at times of crisis and regain the habit. There are, for example, smokers who quit for several months, but as soon as they encounter a crisis, they light one up and go back to their old ways. They light one, thinking that once the crisis is over they'll quit again. But then, habit makes them light one more, and another one, until they go back to being smokers. Nail biting is the same: You bite one nail, and then move on to the other, until all your fingernails are gone.

It's important to go through every exercise and all the book's chapters, since the process is one of maturation, to the point when we are ready to let our nails be whole, healthy and beautiful. Think about it - a fetus born five months into pregnancy would not survive. Nature does not reward anything for being impatient. On the contrary, each process we go through in life has its place; walking the road could be as important as reaching its end. The time it takes to build this process has meaning, which are reflected in its consequence.

My experience as a former smoker, after years of seeing nail biters and working with them, and as a senior theta-healer, has inspired me to sit at my desk and write an interactive book, in which the reader processes the material and makes it inseparable from their reality - from the will to stop biting to complete abstinence. Each chapter is followed by several exercises that illustrate the subject. For the most part, this book presents a variety of reasons for why people bite, "excuses", and of course - solutions. I encourage you to read all the way to the final chapter, and not attempt to stop biting before it is through. I would love to hear of your personal experience, as well as your comments or questions. At the end of the book you'll find contact information. I eagerly await your feedback!

Introduction

Throughout the book we shall look at reasons for nail biting, what it gives us, and the question of whether it benefits or harms us. I am certain that you can find yourself in at least one of these chapters.

I believe that in every habit, whether good or bad, we gain something, and that the habit makes us feel like it's on our side. The book describes how nail biting can help concentration, reduce boredom, calm nerves and cover over guilt, as well as why children bite their nails, and why men and even senior businessmen also have this habit.

We will examine the causes and/or benefits of nail biting, and determine whether it is genetic or actually treatable. The book is packed full of efficient exercises to turn non-beneficial habits into beneficial ones, tips on nail biting and insights into how anyone can stop biting their nails!!!

This is an important, practical book, and it's crucial that you write down every significant lesson you learn along the way. We will go through a joint process for quitting the habit of nail biting. Thus, it's important to read the book in its proper order, and only try to stop biting after you're finished.

It is also vital to read the book once and then repeat it, and to read and perform every exercise. The repetition affects the process we go through in life. Normally, the internalization process occurs on the second or even third read-through of the book. What makes this book unique is its absolute practicality. In this book you find simple and useful methods and formulas that you can easily implement in your daily lives.

The information in this book is based on personal knowledge and experience that I gained in my ongoing journey, researches, client experiences, theta-healing and from people I've met who disclosed their knowledge to me.

This book is meant for people who bite deep, to the flesh, until it hurts. It was meant to convey the meaning of biting, and the cause of it. What makes someone continue the habit of putting their finger in their mouth despite pain, despite shame due to the way their hands' appear, and despite remarks about aesthetics? This book was written to help those who wish to be more-conscious, and combine action with solutions.

At the end of each chapter are exercises. You choose between two options:

One - solve the exercises, write answers on a page and read them after finishing the book to recollect solutions and insights.

Two - Finish the entire book and then return to the exercises. Constant repetition is the name of the game, for each process and area you want to change in your life. Repeating ideas, even if they were already uttered once, take on a different shade and moves into another level of awareness when doing it the second and third time.

Chapter 1

The Main Function of Fingernails

What is the fingernails' main function is a question that any nail biter should ask. If you ask a nail biter what they are fearful or apprehensive about most would not understand the question, since they are unaware that they are destroying their layer of protection.

A nail is a segment of hard tissue at the ends of our hands and feet. Nails are laid of the last cylinder of the finger surface. Their purpose is to protect the nail beds under it.

In fact, the part that's available for biting is the part which can be cut or filed. Some only bite that part, but those who choose to read this book probably bite more than what they're "allowed".

If we walk outside in the winter, when it's cold or snowing, naturally we would wear many layers of insulation. We wouldn't dare remove the protection offered by our clothes, but that's exactly what we do when we bite our nails. The act of biting removes the layer that protects our nails, and protecting the nails is very important. Most biters reach the skin that's under the nail's hard layer, thus causing constant pain. It can be equated to the frost bite we would suffer if we took off our clothes and went for a walk outside in the cold.

If we take a minute before biting our nails to imagine that we would suffer frost bite, would we still bite? Would we eliminate our layer of protection?

Exercises:
- **In which aspects of your life would you**
- **like to feel safer?**

- **In which aspect of your life would you**
- **like to be stronger?**

Chapter 2

Can Nail Biting be Controlled?

Can anyone quit biting? Does the biter control the biting or does it control him/her? Do we act consciously or without thinking? Do we act out of instinct, as in, something is happening and we react without thinking "Wait a minute, is this true? Can this help me?"

Most of the time, people act automatically, out of urges or instinct, similarly to driving. I witnessed this in the year 2000. I was driving my car within the speed limit, calm and relaxed, maintaining a safe distance from other motorists, when the truck driver in the middle lane decided to make a sudden U-turn in the middle of the freeway. Right away, automatically, my foot stepped hard on the brake even though I did not check the rear view mirror to see if there are other vehicles behind me that might hit my rapidly decelerating car. In such conditions, when a stimulus of imminent danger occurs; we react immediately, instinctively and automatically. It's like a worried mother who loses sight of her child, then screams at him not to leave her sight when she finds him again. That is how we react to most of life's events - automatically. You know the cliché, "when angry, count to ten before you speak"? Any event or stimulus triggers an automated, immediate and powerful reaction, just like when I slammed my foot on the brake to prevent hitting the truck.

If we only give some thought to those actions, we can achieve our desired result. And what does this have to do with nail biting? Everyone that I ask "why do you bite your nails?" has automatically answered "I don't know!" Why is this? Can we understand our actions before we act? We can train our thought to serve us. We can constantly know what action to perform, just as soon as we disconnect from automatic thinking and begin thinking logically.

So, why do we bite our nails?

Does the thought precede the biting? A thought that now is the time to bite? Certainly not! It is a completely automatic and thoughtless action. So imagine what would happen if you were to think for a moment, right before you put your finger in your mouth. And no, this does not imply an order not to put your finger in your mouth. Put it in, but just before you do, try and think: Why am I putting my finger in my mouth? Sometimes it happens in times of boredom or watching TV. Sometimes watching TV requires concentration, when you feel it would help you focus on the movie. Is this really true?

Sometimes the biting evokes anger at oneself or at another person. Think of what is the point in biting? Will it alleviate the anger? Will that other person change because you bite your nails to make the anger go away? Will nail biting solve the problem that makes you angry at yourselves? Or is it the other way around - once you put your finger in your mouth, you create new angers, which raises the question of why was I even biting? And why do my fingers look like this? So the initial anger creates additional internal angers.

If we would only stop to think a second before starting to bite, one second before putting a finger in our mouths, we would find the reason for biting. I've heard from several biters that they do it because it's fun. Do you find yourselves thinking, a second before biting, "this is fun, I'm going to enjoy myself now, I'll just put a finger in my mouth and start biting,"? Does that really happen? Is biting fun? One second before you put your finger in your mouth - and again, this is not a suggestion not to put it in, on the contrary! But a second before, just think!!!

It's the thought that counts: Why am I putting my finger in my mouth? Start thinking and be conscious, neutralizing the automatic action and beginning to control your actions. That is the way to produce amazing results in the process.

Anyone can stop nail biting. This method is easy an intuitive, if we only realize that it depends on thought.

Take a second of thought before each action. A second of thought before the finger goes in.

I have a lovely client who used to be a vice-principal in a junior high school. She is a very intelligent woman so I asked her why she bites her nails. Her answer was "I don't know!" Would you believe that such an intellectual woman, who knows so much about life - she was both a senior teacher and a vice-principal at the school - would answer "I don't know"? It's interesting to think how she would feel or react if she asked one of her students "why did you do that?" and that student would answer with "I don't know." and genuinely not know. I believe her that she doesn't know, since she herself never gave a moment of thought before putting the finger in her mouth and never asked herself "Wait a minute, why am I putting my finger in my mouth?" or "What am I gaining from putting my finger in my mouth?"

One evening, I was attending a theater performance with a good friend. At the time, he had something else on his mind, so he automatically put his hand in his mouth during the play. I asked him why his finger was in his mouth and he answered "Oops, I hadn't noticed that..."

That is what happens when we act automatically instead of thinking before doing.

In this chapter, we've seen how we act, discovered that we act automatically and don't stop for a moment before initiating an action, and thus our lives lack self-control. These (automatic) habits have a significant role in our lives; in some cases they are good for us, and in others they slow us down. The habits in our lives can turn into cages, which keep us inside. When we live through our habits, our lives become, literally, habitual. In a way, we become robots, acting automatically: We have an automation that makes us go to work; an automation that makes us sit down to watch the news on TV at 8PM (or any other show); we have an automation that makes us react to the person cutting us in line (or in traffic) and an automation that makes us stop our kids when they fight.

It is for good reason that we stick to our habits. They make us feel safe. We are always more comfortable staying within familiar and safe areas rather than trying new paths toward the unknown.

The moment you feel the need to start biting, wait one second and perform the following two exercises. After that you can resume biting.

Exercises:
Every time you put your finger in your mouth, just before you bite the nail - and I stress that you're allowed to bite - just make sure:
- **Why am I biting?**
- **Would it do me any good?**

Think what you can do instead of biting:
- **Can I do it something else?**
- **How would I feel if I didn't bite?**
- **How would I feel if I did bite?**

Chapter 3

"It's Genetic"

This chapter discusses genetics and hereditary habits, and asks the question is nail biting a matter of nature or nurture? Some of the answers I get when asking "Why do you bite your nails?" were "It's hereditary," "it's genetic," "my mom also used to bite," "It's what I grew up with."

Genetics deal with the transference of attributes from parent to offspring and genetic material is composed of units called genes. Every living creature carries genes that determine its physical body, its physical ability and its behavior. Genes are passed on from generation to generation and determine the common attributes, for individuals of the same gender and for every individual in the population.

A long series of genes make up a chain that is known as DNA. Each gene is responsible for a specific attribute. The various genes are divided into two categories: fixed genes and variable genes. The fixed genes determine bone structure, height, eye color and skin type. These attributes cannot be changed, since the genes responsible for them are fixed. On the other hands, varying genes are the person's "design". Some examples are temper, emotionality, creativity or other character traits.

People inherit both fixed and variable genes. The fact that they are genetic does not mean that they cannot be changed from time to time, according to need.

A large part of our traits are passed to us from our parents, grandparents or other ancestors. These traits can be changed when they are revealed as harmful. For example, if a father passed on to his son a short temper or hypersensitivity, it doesn't mean that the son is unable to change these genetic character traits and live a better and healthier life than his father.

We are a product of the thought habits of ourselves, our family and the people that surround us. Our mental structure, which has accustomed us to bite our nails and dictates our thoughts, feelings and actions toward ourselves and others, is in fact an "unwelcomed present" that we receive from our parents, teachers and other authority figures we encounter.

Our lives are motivated by the thinking mind, the five senses and six intellectual abilities. Everything else is motivated by the subconscious mind, which runs our lives unaware. The thinking mind is the part that exerts discretion. This is where our free will exists. The conscious part of us is what can accept or reject any idea. There is no person or circumstance that can make us think thoughts or receive ideas that we did not choose ourselves. The ideas we choose determine the course of our lives. Pain, pleasure or limitations are created in the conscious mind or have been received from the outside without thinking or using discretion.

Once we have accepted an idea, it is imprinted in the other part of our mind, the subconscious. The subconscious is the source of power and functions in every cell of our body. Every idea that the conscious part chooses to accept, must be received by the subconscious, which cannot reject it.

The subconscious operates in an orderly, lawful manner. It expresses itself through emotions and actions. Every idea and thought that we choose to consciously accept and imprint in our subconscious becomes a part of our personality.

The term "habits" expresses the ideas established in the subconscious, which continue to manifest themselves unassisted by the conscious part, until they are replaced. Every habit we choose to accept can be changed, by choice. Habits are not hereditary. The novel part here is the idea of "mind research" that enables us to take control of our lives and change every habit as we see fit.

Countless times, I've heard "That's just the way I am," "That's how it is," "I can't stop biting my nails." Saying this declares that this is the truth that we believe. And as mentioned, these beliefs are merely the opinions of others, which we have internalized and added to our set of beliefs.

The solution to any bad habit is the decision to change it. Many people fall short on this point. It's hard for them to make such a decision.

I have a client which comes in once every two weeks to refill her French manicure, who has proven to herself more than once that she cannot keep her nails intact (she bites her extensions). In one of the session I asked her: Make a decision and commit to it, out loud, in my presence, that this time you will take care of your nails and that in two weeks you will come back here with nails intact. The client could not commit or make that decision.

To summarize the subject of the biting person's excuses: Every belief we plant in our subconscious has consequences. The biting person too can change their belief that they cannot stop biting, to a belief that they can stop. If one person can do it, then we know it's possible, and all that's left is to find out how.

Once we understand that genetics determine eye color, height, hair color, skin type, etc., we will realize that any behavior can be changed and we can free our lives from negative behavior patterns.

When you feel you want to start biting your nails, wait a second and perform both exercises.

Exercises:

*   The best way to activate your subconscious is through assertiveness and persuasiveness. When you feel physically or mentally distressed, the best thing you can do is let go, and silence your thoughts. Speak to your subconscious. Tell it to take control over serenity. Keep talking to it assertively and persuasively. After this exercise you can resume biting your nails.

*   In the following pages, write down every habit you've changed in your life, things you didn't imagine possible, but succeeded anyway. You can also choose examples from friends or family members and write down what they managed to change.

Chapter 4

"I Can't Focus without It"

In this chapter, we'll discover how nail biting can "contribute" to the biter. Can biting help a person concentrate? To be more attentive and focused?

Many of the people I've asked about why they bite answered that "I bite because it helps me focus," whether it was students who need to focus in school or adults as they read a book or watch television. It was hard for me to understand how biting assists concentration, since as a smoker, I've never smoked for concentration.

"Concentration is a focusing of attention, consideration and effort on a single thing. Attention is focused hearing, listening, consideration for what's being said, while consideration is a "dedication of thought" and observation. All of these are conscious processes during which information reaches the human consciousness through the various senses. It should be emphasized that attention in the sense discussed here ("consideration") is not specifically related to hearing, and we can be attentive to and sensual information.

Can nail biting really assist concentration?

It turns out that it can.

I've asked a life coach who specialized in teens with attention disorders, what should one do when they lose attention, e.g. in a lecture or a conversation with friends. He gave me the following solution: Keep your fingers busy in doodling during the lecture, play with a pen and run it over and over through your fingers, or hold a stress ball and play with it. I asked him "why does that work?" He explained that when the brain has to focus on a specific subject, keeping it busy with a small issue forces it to find concentration on the bigger issue. I did receive an answer, but didn't really understand how it can help. What does it all mean? I went home to try and see if this solution can help me. Would I be more attentive to people if I keep my fingers busy? One day, while treating a client who was an expert on attention and concentration disorders, I told her about my attention issue. She uses different treatment methods, thus her answer was different. I told her about the conversation with the aforementioned friend and while we talked, I told her that the weird thing is that when I work with my clients; I listen with great concentration and also remember all their stories. Dozens of clients a day, and I remember every story. I know I have attention issues and still, when I'm with my clients I find that my attentiveness is at its peak. It was then that I realized that during this time, I'm always doing something with my fingers. I'm a manicurist, so I work with my fingers all the time. I'm manicuring, waxing, doing eyebrows or removing hair - my fingers are always busy with something.

If we recall the life coach's solution, it seems that when the hands are busy with one thing, something in our brain helps us focus on another, bigger issue. I work with my hands, and after so many years, I do it so automatically that I don't need to focus on what I'm doing, thus I have no need to doodle. My entire consideration is given to a client, who is there for the treatment, but also for me to listen to their stories or problems. When I'm with clients, my hands are busy, so my attention is divided between my hands and the client; I'm more focused that way.

Therefore, instead of biting or smoking, you just need to keep your hands busy with something else: A pen, a ball, or just doodling on paper if there is some available.

In this chapter, we've discovered how nail biting assists or contributes to the biter, and how fiddling around with the nails or the skin around them can help the biter focus on another activity. We've also seen the solution to this problem.

Exercises:

- Pay attention, right before you bite, to why you have such a strong urge to put a finger in your mouth, or to fiddle with your nails?

- Buy a small ball or a sketch pad, and while watching TV or listening to the professor, keep your fingers busy with something else and see what happens - do you still miss biting your nails?

Chapter 5
"But I'm Bored!"

What is boredom and why does nail biting take its place?

One of the more common answers I hear to the question "Why do you bite your nails?" is "boredom". It's interesting to examine why people bite when they're bored. Does biting alleviate boredom? Does it fill the time? And what happens later, when it's "not boring"?

Boredom is emptiness, sensory limpness, sadness and indifference, mostly due to idleness or disinteresting content. Boredom is a negative feeling that exists in most mammals, emanating from a lack of stimuli, both physical and emotional. Boredom can also emerge from monotonous activity. Does this interpretation make sense to you? What happens to this negative emotion when we direct our attention from boredom to nail biting? During my smoking days, it took me three minutes to finish a cigarette. When I asked myself, while smoking, "Sarit, why are you smoking right now?" I answered that "I'm bored." It made me feel pathetic, because, well, it's been three minutes. Now what?

This is the question I asked myself every time I felt a need to smoke after I decided to quit: "Common Sarit, so you smoked a cigarette and your three minutes of "fun" that alleviated the boredom. Three minutes have gone by, and that's it! Was it worth it? Is it really worth it to fall off the wagon for three non-boring minutes, which don't really fill the time, but just occupy your mind for a bit giving it three minutes of silence in the internal dialogue, which fills it with things I don't necessarily want to hear, think or feel?"

It all begins and ends with our internal dialogue, the one we'd like to tune out like an annoying song playing on the radio. Imagine that you could just change a channel in your brain, or turn up or down what goes on through our mind. Just like on the radio, we play ourselves all sorts of talks, songs, ideas, etc. All of this occurs in our conscious mind. It's like sitting in front of the TV and rapidly changing channels, without even looking at what's on. That's what we want to be able to do to the thoughts in our heads. The boredom we feel, during which we bite our nails, is similar to watching a disinteresting or uninformative show.

Most of the people that I ask, when do they bite, answer "In front of the TV." A moment later they say they only bite when they're bored. The interesting thing is the relation between nail biting and boredom. While TV is the thing that's supposed to alleviate boredom, it turns out that the biter thinks he bites out of boredom, when in fact, biting does not alleviate boredom, but perhaps increases concentration.

After quitting smoking, you suddenly can't figure out what to do with your fingers, which adds to the urge to light a cigarette - keeping your fingers from getting bored. This is was before I've checked and asked myself, why am I doing this? What good does it do me?

I was completely convinced that boredom was my main reason for smoking cigarettes and that if I smoked, time would go by faster and I wouldn't be bored. I never imagined that it was in order to silence my internal dialogue, or that I'm afraid to spend a moment of silence with myself.

As a former smoker, I noticed that I smoked most of my cigarettes when in my car, especially when waiting at a traffic light or stuck in traffic. When I started noticing nail biters, I saw that they have their hands in their mouths when stuck in traffic, or at a traffic light.

I'm supposed to be my own best friend, and feel good about myself. And what did I do each time I put a cigarette in my mouth? I just grew further away from myself. When I smoked or bit my nails, I was actually stopping my internal dialogue, instead of seeing and understanding what really bothers me. Instead of looking deep into my thoughts, I silenced them with a cigarette or with biting. When I checked with my nail biting clients what they were going through, I discovered that they too were drifting away from themselves.

A client told me, "I don't feel good about myself, so I usually bite." Obviously, she only explained this to me after I delved with her into the bottom of her biting problem, through an internal investigation which I do with my clients, in theta-healing.

If she was aware that she puts her finger in her mouth when she doesn't want to think or feel, it's likely that she wouldn't have been biting, but would find a different solution to the problem - so she told me.

Another client, a clinical psychologist, answered (the question of when she bites) that she usually does it alone in front of the TV. I asked her also if she's aware that she bites in order to avoid herself, her thoughts or her feelings. She answered that she hasn't thought about it. It's very hard to admit; since we do things for ourselves and most of the time we're sure that we love ourselves. But in fact, we bore ourselves, so we drift away by putting fingers in our mouths.

In this chapter, we've discussed boredom and our need to silence thoughts; our need to fill a void. We discovered how much we drift away from ourselves and that biting doesn't really help us fill the time in which we feel bored.

Exercises:

- If you're the type who bites during driving, just before you put the finger in, play a song you really like and turn it up, but it has to be a favorite song that really lifts your mood.

- If you're the type who bites in front of the TV, just before you put the finger in, turn the TV off for a few minutes and then bite. After that you can turn it back on.

Things to Think About:

Chapter 6
"It Calms Me Down"

In this chapter, we'll discuss a person who soothes themselves by nail biting. What are the definition of soothing and tranquility? Did you know that these words are ambiguous? But everyone uses them! What do people mean when they say "It calms me down"? I can try to give my interpretation of the word. When I smoked, I used to say that I smoke to calm down. I meant that I was so nervous and that my head is so cluttered by anger that all I wanted was to silence the anger and divert my attention from it, so I smoked.

So is nail biting a soothing action?

When I asked my clients, "why do you bite?", at first they answered, much like every biter I know, "I don't know." After I insisted that they look within themselves, I asked them to connect to the emotion which accompanies biting and figure out what biting serves, and they answered "calm." Nail biting gives them a calm sensation. When they have a big test coming, or a conversation with the boss, or when they're annoyed because someone upset them, they bite in order to calm down.

Does nail biting sooth? Or does it distract the mind from the unsettling thoughts?

I remember that when I smoked, I too said that it calms me down and that I can't quit because I'd turn into an irate person. The truth is that perhaps in the beginning, fearful of how I would manage, I thought that I'd be irate. To my surprise, I became calmer. I suddenly noticed that I'm not busy looking for spare minutes between clients to smoke - I used to pray before each session that the client would come early, so that I'd have a few minutes of "fresh air" with a cigarette. When I went to visit my family, I was always asking "when do we leave?" so I could light one up. So, instead of enjoying my time where I was, I was preoccupied with "alright, when do I leave, when can I finally light a cigarette?"

When I was nervous because someone upset or hurt me, I'd smoke a cigarette, thinking that "I need a cigarette to calm down!" Did smoking actually solve a problem for me with that person? Although it is said to be known that the chemicals in the cigarette do affect nerves calming them, in my case at the time, I did not give it much thought and just acted automatically, treating smoking as a sedative. While it's true that biting is slightly different than this case, since in biting there are no chemicals which affect the nervous system, it's still not supposed to "bother" anyone - It doesn't produce malodor or damages the environment or the biter's health.

Some biters relax by biting when they're nervous. And indeed, I asked one of my clients, a stewardess, "Please, just check one second before you bite - don't stop biting, that's not what I ask - just a second before you do, find out why you do it."

She came back with the following answer: "Every time I meant to put my finger in my mouth, I have to admit that I thought about what you said and couldn't bite." I asked her, "So what did you do?" and she answered: "I found myself crying when I'm nervous, and that's how I vented my anger. I found myself talking to the person who hurt and upset me." I loved hearing her solution for finding inner peace.

If she bit, it wouldn't have solved her problem with the person who hurt her. By refraining from biting, she solved two problems at once: She kept her nails pretty and intact, and also solved the issue of the person who hurt her.

In case there is no way of talking to that person and resolving the issue, I'd recommend writing down your anger on a piece of paper, tearing it to shreds and burning it. That's another method for calming down.

Nail biting causes frustration, self-neglect and fingernail neglect, and damages your hands' aesthetic. Contrarily, if you find an alternative solution like that stewardess did, you win twice: Your hands stay well-kept and you create an inner calm.

I have college student clients who bite, and when I asked them why they do, they answered that the stress before a test makes them bite. During class, they put their fingers in their mouths to focus. They told me that they bite when they're stressed about coming tests. When they think about whether they will pass or fail, the biting calms them down. The extensive cramming also puts a lot of pressure on them due to the vast amounts of material and the "unknowns" before the test, so they bite.

I've also seen a successful lawyer, that before every trial where she has to represent a client, she bites her nails down to the flesh, until there's nothing left. She told me that she bites due to the stress of the complicated case that she has undertaken and also because she is uncertain of winning or losing the trial. Here as well - does biting define calmness or the lack of it? That lawyer, who bites her nails or distracts herself from the pressure she's under and translates the biting into relaxation, should ask herself, one second before she puts the nail in her mouth, "Am I really calming down?"

In this chapter, we've seen my definition of calm, since there is no real dictionary definition for it. Is it a mere distraction from those negative emotions which stress us, which are then automatically translated into calmness. We've seen the true reason for "relaxation" and presented several examples of people who associate a calming effect to biting.

Exercises:

- When you feel stressed, one second before you bite, take three deep breaths: While inhaling, imagine that you're letting in light in a color you like, and when exhaling take out all the bad feeling that makes you feel the negative emotion. Then, put your finger in your mouth and start biting.

- When you fell stress or tension, take a piece of paper and write what you feel, whatever goes on in your head during moments anger, stress, tension - take it all out on the paper, and if possible, burn the paper. After you're done, you can start biting the nail.

Chapter 7

Going Guilt-Free

In this chapter, I'll highlight the manner in which guilt affect the nail biter, and how biting contributes to the guilt-ridden person. I'll present examples of people who were driven by guilt to put their fingers in their mouths and bite.

As with each chapter, I'll begin with a dictionary definition for guilt: "The way a person feels when they believe that they have done something wrong, unacceptable or something that does not align with their principles. Normally, when one offends another person or insults them." For example, every mother feels guilt in every interaction with her kids. When they're upset or crying, the mother is flooded by guilty emotions: Am I a good mother? Did I do the right thing? Another example very common among my clients is of those who decided to leave their partner because the relationship didn't seem to fit anymore. The other side got hurt, and what happened to the side that broke it off? They are automatically overcome with guilt: Why did I hurt him/her? I didn't mean to hurt.

Sexual harassment also provides examples, when a woman or girl is sexually exploited. They know that they were wronged, and despite it, the woman or girl usually feels guilty. She knows something bad is happening, she just doesn't know what. This is the same with mental abuse - here too, the guilt rises in the victim rather than in the abuser.

These cases, especially the last ones, are indeed extreme, but the fact is that guilt is felt by every person in existence, mainly vis-à-vis other people, family and friends. This guilt fills us with feelings of inferiority, and many times people deliver negative messages to us because it is the easiest way to manipulate us.

Instead of agreeing to be a victim of manipulation, all we have to do is ask ourselves "Why are they doing this?" and "What do they really want?" The thought precedes the emotion, so if we pay attention to our thoughts, we can control our emotions.

One of my clients complained that she cannot stop biting her nails, and that her daughter, who lives with her, keeps telling her off about it. The daughter says that it's ugly and asks the mother to stop. I asked her why she bites, and she answered "It's beyond my control, it relaxes me, I bite until it hurts." I look at her curiously and asked again "Why?" Her answer: "I always carry with me guilt over something that happened in my family, and when I bite it calms me down."

Guilty feelings are one of the most common reasons for nail biting. The expressions "Eating him up on the inside," is an accurate description for nail biting, since a person cannot literally eat himself, but nail biting is as close as one can get to it. It's self-punishment. If the aforementioned client could have solved her family issues; if she took charge and seen how she could make things better. I she had treated her guilt by talking to family members or a suitable professional, or simply forgive herself, she would not have had to resort to a state of punishment or the need to hurt herself.

This client is one example of nail biting without awareness of its meaning. If this woman was aware that when she bites her nails she is punishing herself and that there are other solutions rather than causing herself pain. I believe that her finger would have never gone in her mouth. Perhaps, temporarily, biting resolved the guilty feeling, but after she was done biting her nails raw, there was no actual release of guilt nor was there a solution to the family issues. After all, the solution is in her head - not in her nails.

Can nail biting be a "happy place" when a person punishes himself in such a way that that they reach self-destruction (although limited) or a feeling that they aren't worthy or good enough?

The guilty feelings are usually accompanied by self-criticism. You know, that inner judge that lives within us, who keeps telling us off berating ourselves. When we condemn ourselves, when we "hit" ourselves? Who are we actually addressing? Who are we criticizing?

After the self-deprecation stage, the contemplation stage and the inner dialogue stage, comes the action stage - smoking or nail biting.

Two of my friends broke up, and the man told the woman that she's the one who caused the breakup and that if she would have picked up his signals, they wouldn't have broken up. The woman, a nail biter, what do you suppose she did after that accusation? She bit her nails raw until there was barely any nail left. If she would have asked herself if a breakup can be blamed exclusively on one side, perhaps she would have understood what happened (there are two sides to every breakup), and try to work on what she was to blame for in the breakup. She would have taken responsibility of her actions, and at the same time forgiven herself for her mistakes in the relationship as to not repeat them. I believe that her guilt would have been gone and the nails would not have been an issue.

I state again that this book was written out of my own experience in quitting smoking. Are cigarettes not self-destructive? We use smoking, among other things, to relieve our guilt? How many people consciously damage their health, but are unaware that at the moment of putting the cigarette in their mouths, they feel guilt and want to destroy themselves? How many people bite their nails and dislike themselves because of the way their hands look. Yet, they continue to bite, unaware that they are closing themselves in a cage of guilt, instead of forgiving themselves?

Children are a good example, when discussing people who punish themselves. Children make a lot of mistakes, they test the limits of our patience, and many times we are angry at them yet we still forgive them (this is an example regarding the adult's side in the matter. Although the adult forgives the child, the child might interpret the anger as a grave offense - but here I would like to present a message of forgiveness, about how we can easily forgive our children, but not so much ourselves). Why do we not forgive ourselves? Why do we continue not forgiving ourselves and punishing ourselves with guilt? Even when we punish a child, we "let go" after a few minutes, forgive them and explain the proper way to behave. Why is it that for ourselves, we do not internally explain the proper way, and make amends? Even when we can't turn back the wheel, like repairing an heirloom that the child broke - do we treat them with the same severity that we treat ourselves?

Inside each of us is a child, one that needs our love and forgiveness. If you become aware that when you are angry at yourself, you're actually angry at that inner child and I believe you'd find it easier to forgive yourself and you won't have to bite you nails raw again. The problem's solution is to understand the underlying reason that we put our finger in our mouth. What is the source of the guilt? Can biting free us of guilt, or solve the problem that makes us feel guilt?

In this chapter, we've seen examples of people who carry around guilt and are too judgmental of themselves and their actions. These are the main causes of nail biting. We've had one example of that small child who misbehaves, and saw the way we treat them. We've seen that we have much more compassion for a child than for ourselves. In the same way that a child needs comforting after punishment, we need it too, since each of us has that child inside.

Exercises:

- **When you feel guilt, take a pen and paper and write down what you feel, if and how you could take responsibility and make amends? If you can't take it back, write yourself an apology letter. After you're done, you can go back to biting you fingers.**

- **Uplifting exercise: Mirrors reflect our emotions regarding ourselves. Every time you feel flooded by guilt, look in the mirror - into your own eyes - and say out loud something positive like "You're a wonderful person," or "I love you despite everything." At the beginning you'd feel a bit irrational, but over time you'll discover how good this makes you feel and you'll start doing it more and more. After you're done, you can go back to biting your fingers.**

- **When you're angry at yourself, imagine that you're angry at a three year old. If you were facing a small, scared child, what would you do? Would you lash out at them or would you reach out your arm and comfort them, until they felt safer? Be kind to yourselves, and start loving and appreciating yourself, and then forgive yourself. After this exercise, you can go back to biting your nails.**

Chapter 8

What to Do with Biting Children?

Our habits are usually acquired at a young age, perhaps even 2-3 years old. How does biting affect children and why do they usually bite? In this chapter, we'll take a look at biting children, the reasons for their biting and the solution to it.

Children are like a sponge; they absorb knowledge from us, their parents, social environment, teachers, TV and other sources of information and influence.
We have tremendous potential to influence our kids, mainly in light of the understanding that influence is not hereditary and it is possible to stop existing habits, specifically nail biting, even before childhood has ended.

Our responsibility as parents is to know what to let our kids absorb, and teach them to let go of what they don't need. It is just as you would squeeze excess water out of a sponge, yet the sponge remains moist.

Adults and children alike don't know how to rid themselves of unnecessary things - anger, fear, worry and angst (which occur in practically every person). Similar to adults, the child searches for ways to avoid them, unknowingly, of course.

That child who can't properly let go of these unnecessary feelings can show many symptoms, such as overeating, becoming violent, isolating themselves by staying in their room watching television or sitting at the computer for longer than is acceptable and, of course, the child can start biting their nails. A child who is unable to share their emotions or their problems looks for ways to silence the noise in their head, noise that causes frustration, fear and even lack of focus. Thus, they translate nail biting into a problem solving method. This is how a nail biting addiction begins. That child finds out that if they put their finger in their mouths or gets busy eating, even when not hungry, their mind are at peace. They aren't preoccupied with angst, anger, frustration... thus they manage to silence the noise in their head. The noise I'm describing here is their internal dialogue: "Did I do well, did I do wrong," "Will mom and dad be angry with me?" "Will this kid be my friend or not?" "Will I pass the test or not?" And these are just some of the thoughts going through their heads.

I've met a ten year old boy who was nail biting in front of me, and I asked him "Why do you bite?" the same way I ask adults, and he told me it's a habit of his from a very young age. I insisted and asked him "Do you know why you bite?" He said "It helps me think," and this was exactly one hour before he was supposed to receive an answer on whether he won a Lego contest or not. He added, "For example, now I'm biting because I'm nervous. I tried stopping a few times, but every time I went back to biting." In the same conversation, his mother said that she too has been biting since the age of four, when she immigrated to Israel and didn't speak Hebrew. The other children made fun of her. She was really frustrated about not knowing the language and about dealing with the kids around her, so she started putting her finger in her mouth and biting. Instead of learning to speak, she just plugged her mouth with her finger. In fact, there can be various reasons for biting (conscious and subconscious). One - the child imitates his mom's biting; two - the child bites due to stress, or is afraid to speak.

One day, a client came to my clinic with her son, a 13 years old, brilliant boy. I could tell from his questions that he was very intelligent. While treating his mother, I could see him putting his finger in his mouth, so I asked him if he bites his nails. He answered, "Of course, I've been biting since I was little. I love biting my nails." I asked him why, his reply was, "it makes me feel good." A 13 year old who cannot differentiate conscious from subconscious, knows that if he feels bad and puts his finger in his mouth, it makes him feel better. A 13 year old, when he feels that the dialogue in his head makes him uncomfortable, believes that if he puts his finger in his mouth it would solve his "problems", and that he would feel better about himself. What actually happens is the child becomes addicted to biting instead of talking about his problems.

Since his mind is preoccupied with biting, he was no ability to think at that moment about something else, and "peace" is created in his mind. That is how he concluded that biting solves the problem and is like water being squeezed from a sponge.

I asked that child, "Try to explain it to me anyway, why is it good for you?" He answered that he bites mostly when he needs to concentrate. From here, it was clear how much this child needed to silence his inner dialogue, how desperately he needed concentration and was unable to break free of the noise by himself.

The way to help the children whose heads are filled with noise, is to simply talk to them. Talk to them like you're sharing, like we adults share with our friends or even professionals when something bothers us, when we're angry, afraid or frustrated.

You should present the child with open-ended questions: "What's going on with you?" and not closed-ended ones such as "Are you upset?" One should encourage the children to speak and not ask general questions, like "How was your day?" but really dig deep and ask "What did you do at recess? How were the other kids? Did something unpleasant happen with a friend or a teacher?"

The goal is to allow the child to express themselves and vent emotions, without judgment or response. Instead of the dialogue staying internal, the child should feel that they can let out emotions or angst and talk about what's going on, instead of keeping quiet with their fingers and nails. A child who manages an inner dialogue which makes them uncomfortable will do anything to stop feeling bad, and the whole point is to let the child express their emotions.

Some psychologists say that children have a hard time expressing their feelings, and should be encouraged to do so through various arts such as writing, drawing and sculpting. These are all instruments that can help them express or vent emotions, or as we describe it, release the inner dialogue. Some say sports are effective as well, since expending energy also releases emotion.

These solutions can help when trying to get a child to quit nail biting, presenting him with alternative solutions until they accustom themselves to stop biting. But these solutions won't be useful for long if the parent doesn't understand that the child puts their finger in their mouth because they want to silence or release their inner dialogue. Once the child begins to talk about what goes on in their mind, they would feel safe around their parents and teachers, knowing that they can always share with others and release their inner dialogue, and then the biting will be gone for good!

On a personal note, my son, who's 3 years old today, puts his finger in his mouth, and I ask him the same open-ended question, with one close-ended question at the beginning for direction: "Are you upset?" and then a dialogue begins, which includes question about why, who and what would he want to happen instead. Then, without noticing, he just removes the finger from his mouth and doesn't put it back after venting his emotions. I noticed that when we sit in front of the TV and has his finger in his mouth, and I ask him "What's in your mouth?" he answers "Nothing!" and immediately takes it out, so that each time the finger goes in, I encourage him to talk and share and it really worlds. Even before I decided to write this book, I saw evidence that my son is going to be a nail biter, so every time I told him to take his finger out, he would leave it in to spite me. Since writing the book and performing the exercises with my son, I see that it simply works: There is no more being spiteful and he removes his finger very easily. I see fewer and fewer occurrences over time.

As with every chapter, I have some exercises for you.

Exercises:
- **When you notice that one of your children begins putting their finger in their mouth, encourage them to talk about what they feel, share with them and teach them how to share their emotions.**

- **If one of your children bites in front of the TV, ask them what they have in their mouth and pay attention to their behavior.**

- **When you see that one of your children bites in order to concentrate, buy them a soft ball to play with in their hand; it should be the size of the palm and not make any noise. Guide them to squeeze it during times of stress or angst, thus releasing sensations, thoughts, anger, frustrations and emotions.**

Chapter 9

The Closeted Biter

In this chapter, we'll discuss those people who do not admit to their addiction to nail biting, those people who think that if no one sees them doing it; then it doesn't really happen. Among smokers, it's very common to smoke secretly and then chew gum or use breath spray to mask the smell of the cigarette.

We hide what we believe others would perceive as negative. We hide what we think is abnormal, but most of all, we hide our hidden desires. If they're hidden, we assume that they deviate from the acceptable norm.

Shame isn't, therefore, a clear and absolute value, but a subjective one which is open for interpretation and adjustment based on the individual's opinion of themselves and the way they are perceived by others.

Shame is a concept very common in our cultural and moral existence from very early on: In the story of the Garden of Eden, before eating the forbidden fruit (Tree of the Knowledge of Good and Evil), it was written: "And they were both naked, the man and his wife, and were not ashamed." After eating the forbidden fruit and hiding from God, Adam said unto God: "...I heard Thy voice in the garden, and I was afraid, because I was naked; and I hid myself."

"Living without shame" is a bi-polar reality: The positive, inherent to an individual's ability to live their lives through introspection and lack of judgment or comparison to the environment and its norms; living out of inner truth - being naked - without concealing or covering up their essence and identity. The negative, surprisingly, is the very result at the foundation of the intent. Living a lie and concealing, avoiding judgment, in order to create a virtual reality, which allegedly suits society's opinions and norms.

Some people eat in secret; when no one is around, the sneak to the fridge and start binging. I've heard of a phenomenon of people who eat during sleepwalking, some of them not even aware that they eat in this manner. These people are afraid to admit, to themselves and their friends, that they're addicted to food.

The nail biters have the same habit: One they're alone in front of the TV or computer, they start biting. When I speak to these people, they confess their clandestine habits. "I'm not addicted, I do it sometimes when I'm alone in front of the TV," is what a very classy and sophisticated client, a psychologist by vocation, told me. To her, if she bites alones, it doesn't count as an addiction.

I know another person who said, "When I sit at the computer, only during work, it just bothers me; the pieces of skin or the uneven nail, and I have to even it out." I wonder what that means. - when a person is around others, does the uneven nail not bother them? Neither do the hangnails? Then why does it bother him when he's alone?

The shame of biting nails around people is profound. The feeling of "What do they think of me or say about me" troubles a lot of people, who can't just admit out load: "I'm addicted!!!"

During my smoking days, I always used to say about myself that I'm not addicted and that I can quit anytime. I used to state that I've stopped smoking, and I would really stop, through willpower. After a few months I would go back but not immediately tell everyone about it. Mostly, I would smoke in secret and carry packs of gums or mints in my bag so people won't know I fell off the wagon. The shame of being so weak that I cannot live up to my commitment to stop smoking was deep. The thought that I had to sneak away just to smoke cigarettes made me feel like a criminal, having to steal moment for myself so that no one would find out. This habit of hiding me or the cigarettes was very burdensome. Even to myself, I could not admit that I was an addict!!! So, I smoked my cigarettes secretly until the need to smoke became greater and greater, so I slowly began hinting at my cohorts that I wanted to go back to smoking. They said "But you've already stopped and haven't smoked in a while (nine months at maximum), wouldn't it be a shame to go back now?" I'd excuse it with all sorts of reasons, since I was already back to smoking, just secretly... so I went back to smoking thinking that at least I managed to cut down.

I can tell you that it lasted exactly one month, (the statement that I was only smoking a few cigarettes a day), and pretty soon I was back to smoking a pack a day, until I discovered the method to quitting smoking. I've been cigarette-free since 2006, and I'm certain that I'll never go back to smoking.

During my first attempts to stop smoking, I was very proud of myself for succeeding and would tell all my friends that I don't smoke anymore. When I would fall off the wagon or bum a smoke from a friend, just to relax or feel like one of the gang at the moment, it would make me want to take another puff and then another, thus I went back to smoking, but not publicly. No way, after I said to everyone that I've stopped? So I'd always smoke alone and then chew some gum or use some breath spray to cover up my habit. When it finally got to bothersome to hide it, I officially announced that I went back to smoking!

In the past, I would always go back to smoking because I didn't realize how addicted I was, just like an alcoholic. I told myself that I can quit anytime, so I'd quit when I want to. I didn't realize it was a part of a cycle. I only internalized what quitting meant when I understood that I'm not allowed even a single drag, like an alcoholic who cannot even have a sip of sacramental wine.

At first I thought it took self-control, but what is self-control anyway? After all, we're in some form of control all day long: When we're driving and the speed limit is 50, we won't drive 100 if we feel like it at the moment. Or if we want to go on vacation but can't afford it right now, we'll manage our funds and not buy a plane ticket to Thailand.

We drive the speed limit even though sometimes we want to go faster, because we know that if we break the law we'll pay a heavy toll. That is what we were taught as children.

What price do we pay when we bite or smoke? One may say that we pay a price in our health if we smoke or bite deep and injure ourselves, which is also detrimental to health. And still, some smokers continue to smoke even after multiple heart attacks, or bite despite the fingers becoming infected and swollen. The biter can attest to the excruciating pain this causes, and despite the toll it takes, they keep biting.

So where is this so-called control? Can we really control ourselves? What we can do is ask ourselves a very simple question - "Does biting do me good?"

Closet smokers are considered casual smokers, ones that don't need a pack a day like I do, so they don't consider themselves heavy smokers or addicts.

With the closeted biter, things are a bit different since they can't conceal their biting with mints or scented gums. Women can hide it with a French manicure, and men can bite around the nail so the damaged skin is not apparent, buy eventually they're still addicted to the same habit of nail biting. The biter is not compulsive like the two-pack a day smoker and can be considered a casual biter, but they are still an addict.

The idea of admitting first and foremost, before trying to stop biting, smoking, over-eating or any other nasty habit, is to admit to yourself, "I'm an addict!!!"

In summation, even someone who bites secretly at home or just bites the corner of the nail on a regular basis, even if they don't "wipe out" all their nails, must admit to themselves that they are addicted to this habit and realize that there is a solution. They do not need to hide or "steal" a few minutes in private to enjoy nail biting.

Exercises:

- **If you relate to this chapter and are among the closet addicts, I invite you to look in the mirror and say "I'm addicted to nail biting," just like in an Alcoholics Anonymous meeting. Except in this case, you're looking at yourselves in the mirror and confessing. After this exercise, you're may resume biting if you feel like it.**

- **After the first exercise, you should grab a pen and paper, write down "I'm addicted to nail biting", and tape the paper on your closet. The very act of writing or looking at the page generates a change in your awareness, toward meaningful action.**

Things to Think About:

Chapter 10
Why Do Men Bite?

So far, the book has discussed mostly cases of women biters. But this phenomenon does not spare men whatsoever! From senior managers to laborers, men everywhere and throughout history have bitten their nails. The world of male biters is so vast that I must dedicate an entire chapter to it. This chapter is intended for men, since the characteristics of male biters are different than those of women and children biters.

I've chosen to write an entire chapter about men since I realized that a very large percentage of the addict biters are men, and moreover, they cannot use replacements, unlike women who can have a French manicure or hide their nails with nail polish. The frustration I've witnessed in men who do care how their nails look like was significant.

My clients are mostly women. Men don't come to my clinic to get a French manicure. Some men come in for a manicure on occasion, to take care of the skin around the nail. One known phenomenon among biters is the excess skin around the nail. I've had many clients who asked me to build nails for their sons or husbands until they stopped biting. I thought it was a bit too feminine to build nails for men, so at first I tried to offer them my way, even before I discovered the method to quit biting, of using various nibble inhibitors, in the hope that they would stop their biting.

Obviously, the nibble inhibitor method did not work, and today I can say that even if I built their nails it wouldn't have helped, since I've even seen clients biting through their French manicure.

It should be mentioned that male biters are very different from smokers, since smoking is considered very "manly", and a social construct of being "one of the guys". However, nail biting among men is not considered desirable in any way.

In a research I performed, I approached several men and discovered a common denominator in most of them: Nail biting doesn't bother them. In contrast to the women, who are more open to discussing the matter, the men I've interviewed as research for the book didn't admit that biting is an issue for them. Very few men admitted to me, saying "Sarit, I've tried everything, nothing works!" or "Can you build me artificial nails?" I've met a man who lectures to audiences about motivation to success in life. When I asked him if he wanted to stop biting, he answered that "It doesn't get in the way of my success." I asked a CEO of a large organization, "Why do you bite?" He answered, "I bite only when the people I'm with are boring." Another man, who owns a large PR company answered that "I've had this habit for years." Nonetheless, I asked him to consider why he's biting, and told him that I'd call in a few days and that in the meantime he should pay attention to why he's biting; that he can keep biting but I'd like to know what the reason is." After a few days, I called to ask and he answered that "I bite mainly when I read the Globes newspaper. If the articles are interesting then the finger stays out, but when I skip to the part where I already know the subject, or if it's boring, although I don't skip these parts or stop reading, but I bite all my nails to the last finger. That is why I bite." I met a well-known importer and asked him the same question. He answered that "It's a habit, probably hereditary, but it doesn't affect my sales. I'm a go-getter and it doesn't bother me."

A client of mine told me about her husband: When they first met, she saw that he was biting his nails and it somewhat bothered her, until she understood that every time he was angry at her, or in general, he would immediately start biting his nails to the flesh. She tried everything she could to get him to quit, but to no avail. She told me that every time he bit, she would get sick to her stomach, because she knew that "My husband is mad now; it would be a bad idea to go near him right now." This would happen often, and you can imagine such an alienated relationship, in which the woman distances herself from her husband every time she sees him bite, so he won't lash out at her. And, of course, talking to him about it was out of the question.

One day she came to me with eyes shining bright and told me, "He stopped biting, he stopped biting!" I asked her how it happened, and she told me that he got a new job and bought expensive new clothes and shoes. She asked him, "What's the point of having a nice wardrobe if your hands look terrible?" And he hasn't put a finger in his mouth ever since. Thus, he stopped biting and she was happy and unafraid to go near an angry husband who expresses his angers with nail biting.

I asked her, "And how does he relax now? He has to vent his anger somehow..." She said that he started going to the gym and trying to better himself, and has become a more aesthetic, well-kept and of course healthier person. That client's case helped me understand that nail biting is a tell to a person's character: It shows what kind of person they are, whether calm, peaceful, well-kept... nurturing doesn't have to be external, but internal as well. Her husband's story shows us how to combine internal nurturing with external nurturing. Going to the gym made him a healthier person, externally and internally. How does that correspond with looks? Are aesthetics meaningless in the world of men? This world has always fascinated me, so I decided to delve into it, though men were less cooperative on this subject. Although, if we look at the statistics, I'm afraid I'll find that men come in at first place.

I checked online and found out that men constitute 29% out of all biters, who are 44% in total - a significant portion. In this chapter, I reach out to men who want to be self-aware and stop hurting themselves, men who are willing to take a leap of faith without shying away or side-stepping.
This book is intended for men who want to stop being a part of the 29%.

I'll present a relatively small sample of reasons for men's biting, since they were less cooperative. I've no idea why - perhaps they were more timid, or perhaps it truly doesn't bother them. They are certainly not reading this book right now, unless their spouse bought them a copy. I recommend reading all chapters and performing the exercises.

Most men I've seen bite in cars, when stuck in traffic, at a stop light, in bars, men I've met in dates and in all sorts of business meetings. In my field, I meet mostly women because they are the ones who come into my clinic, but when I go out to take a class or group activity, I see men biting in the crowd. Some of the men I meet at a lecture or just casually show their bite-ridden nails when we shake hands. Some men completely damage their skin because they bite the flesh around the nail itself.
I can't always ask these men as to the reason of the biting, but when I do, I'm not always met with cooperation. For the most part, men are introverted and cannot admit to having a problem out loud.

One man whom I met after beginning work on the book told me that he bites from a very young age. When he's at work, he doesn't bite since he's busy, and only begins biting at home, where it's quiet. He shared with me that he tried to stop biting several times but the tension which built up in his body drove him mad, and he was preoccupied all day long with the thought of going back to biting. He used his willpower, and obviously he gave in at some point and went back to biting. He noticed that he bites because he doesn't even notice he's doing it, but his feeling after he's done biting was quite unpleasant. He told me: "I

work with people, and feel bad when I have to expose my hands."
Another man, I interviewed, told me that every time he gets into
an argument with his spouse, he finds himself first eating he skin
around the nail, until he reaches the nail itself, and only then starts
to even out the nail and then biting all of it. This continues until the
fight stops, after which he is bummed out by falling off the wagon
again.

There's another nice young man who told me that he quit through
sheer willpower, but every so often he evens out a protruding
corner because of the sensation he gets when it touches his hand.
He goes back to biting and then stops periodically. So he starts
biting or stops when he feels like it.

When we act out of willpower, we give in at crisis moments and
return to the habit, whether it's biting, overeating, or smoking.
Willpower is useful when combined with an awareness of "Why
I'm doing what I'm doing," replacing the habit with another, positive
element.

In summation, when we examined the world of addicted biters, we
saw that a very large percentage of the biter population is men. The
solution to the problem in biting men is slightly more complicated
than the one for women, since they cannot have artificial nails
built. We've seen that the vast majority of men are uncooperative.
Some are cooperative those who aren't really bothered by their
habit of nail biting.

Exercises:

- For what reason do you want to stop biting? It's important to set a goal - why even stop biting?

- After reading every chapter and discovering the reason for biting, look for one or two habits you have and turn them into positive habits (for example, you've discovered that you bite for concentration. Take a chain of beads or a soft object and start manipulating it with your hand when you lose focus.) Now, after performing the exercises, you may go back to biting.

Chapter 11

What does it Feel Like to Stop Biting?

After years of biting, people say to themselves that they like biting nails and that they cannot stop. But all of a sudden, after they've decided to stop completely, they see what a wonderful feeling quitting brings them, and the aesthetic feeling brings them joy.

Below are some quotes of people who quit biting their nails:

"It feels wonderful!"

"I can finally wear my rings!"

"I sit all day long and look at my hands with excitement. You wouldn't believe how often that happens. When I drink coffee, I look at my fingers holding the mug. When I'm in the bathroom, when I smoke, I look at them and feel like a movie star, I can't believe I have nails, and long ones at that.

"I can finally get a French manicure."

"Me having nails??? That's unbelievable!"

"I can go to business meetings without having to pocket my hands."

"Since I have nails, I feel much more confident."

"It's so much fun that I can go without biting at all, I didn't believe it was possible."

"My old friends are impressed by me having long nails."

"It's so much fun having long and aesthetic nails that I can coat with red nail polish."

"I'm so happy, now that I have pretty, well-kept nails."

"Finally, I have natural, long nails, so I don't need artificial ones anymore."

"When I stopped biting, I got a French manicure and it was beautiful, so I decided that's how I want my hands to always look! Today I'm grossed out by people who bite!"

"I was so disgusted at my nails, but today I feel great. I am confident and pleased to shake hands with my clients."

I remember that when I stopped smoking after so many years, I was thrilled that I didn't need a cigarette in my hand. At first, I hung out with smokers and craved the smell of cigarettes, as if I was smoking. But over time, when I would recall smoking, I couldn't figure out why I wanted to smoke. Today, I'm glad that habit is behind me and that I don't smoke anymore. The aesthetic aspect plays a major role, since there is no smoky smell on my skin, clothes, hair or hands. I've heard of similar feelings from former biters.

"It feels very clean."

"I feel aesthetic and groomed."

"I feel very feminine."

"I don't even get why I needed it. The important thing is that it's behind me!"

In summation, though the examples I presented were mostly of women, I believe that if I had asked more men, they would've answered in a similar manner. There are no benefits to biting and it contributes nothing. The feeling you get after quitting biting is wonderful and should be felt by all biters. I've decided to quote several examples in order to spur people to quit biting and show what those who quit gained by it. This way, you can begin to imagine what will happen after your withdrawal. Imagining this can improve your feeling and advance your withdrawal process.

Exercises:
- Grab a small notebook and write down all your strong suits, e.g.: If you're a good friend, write that you're social! If you tell the truth, write that you're honest! At least 15 strong suits.

- Sit down for five minutes and imagine how you'd feel or act once you've stopped biting. Write how your day would look like without biting and what you would gain from it.

After performing these two exercises, you may go back to biting.

Chapter 12

What Does a Biter Look Like to Others?

I've found out that there are two types of people in the world: Those who constantly obsess over what their neighbors might say, and those who don't give a damn about other people's opinion and do whatever they feel like. This chapter discusses the former group, and what they look like to others.

In order to write this chapter, I asked how biters look like from different perspectives: Those of biters and those of non-biters. The answers I got were diverse and surprising even to me.

The non-biters' answers were very subtle. I mostly got "It's unaesthetic," "I've never noticed it," "I dunno, it doesn't bother me," or "It's embarrassing." These were very diplomatic answers given the subject.

When I asked those who don't bite, I got the impression that they did not picture a biter, and that it took them several minutes to think of someone they know who bites, and what they think of them.

The more interesting group was of the biters and former biters. They're answers weren't subtle and standard, instead they were more concise.

We'll start with the easy ones and work out way up.

I had a client who stopped biting because she has artificial nails, but by definition she is still a biter, the same way that in the periods when I stopped smoking - whether because of pregnancy or nursing, I would say that "I don't smoke now, but I'm a smoker." In the same way, that client is certain that if I remove her French manicure, she would go back to biting. This is a client who said that when she sees people biting, she immediately thinks about her son, who's a biter as well, or about her childhood, the time when she started biting. She tells of this with a sweet smile implying a good memory, of somewhere she'd like to go back to.

I asked another client, who has already stopped biting without artificial nails or aids, just by deciding to do it, what she thought about biting people. She said, "A biting person seems to me like they're lost in thought." I asked her why she was biting and it turns out that she was one of those who bite for concentration. She believes that biting would assist her in this. Naturally, I asked her if she can concentrate without biting, and the answer was "Of course I can!"

One of my long-time clients who comes in for French manicures, allows herself to come to me with more than two nails bitten. She told me that she thinks that biters seem like anxious, irritated people. It turns out that in her case the biting is a result of unrest: When she wants peace, she starts biting.

A more moderate answer about biters came from another client: I think they're the most bored people in the world, because when she bit, she usually did it when she was bored or nervous.
I got a lot of answers about what biting adults or children exhibit: Poor character, inability to cope, low confidence, disgusting and unaesthetic, very close personality, unpleasant to be around, so gross.

These answers and similar ones remind me of how I felt after I quit smoking. I looked at smokers almost the same way. In the first rounds of quitting, when I quit by sheer will, I would look at smokers with passion and temptation to go back to smoking. I felt that it was so sexy looking at a woman smoke, but after I quit completely, not just by my will, but through the method I'm writing about in this book, I became a person who doesn't smoke at all and never will. I began seeing smokers as unaesthetic people. I had a hard time being around them because of the smell (at least in biters, since biting doesn't emit any odors).

I felt that a smoking person is an irritated, anxious person, and that's what worked for me - a cigarette to cool down.

I'm certain that nail biters are completely unaware of what they look like. They don't ask themselves at each moment why they bite, or what other people think of them. More importantly, they do not look inward. They bite just because, just like me when I opened my pack and smoked - Just Because.

In summation: To non-biters a biter seems as unaesthetic and neglected and to people who do bite they seem anxious, hesitant, weak of character, unable to cope, of low confidence, disgusting and unpleasant to be around.

Exercises:
- **Take a few minutes of your time and think: Who do you know that bites, and what do you think of them? Write it down in the attached pages.**

- **Take a few minutes of your time and look at yourselves, what would you look like to others, if they were asked about you?**

Write it down in the attached pages.
You may now go back to biting!

Chapter 13
"But I Love Biting!"

This chapter will discuss people who admit that they're addicted to nail biting and do not need or want to hide their habit. They say about themselves, "But I love biting." People who like biting excuse their addiction with their love for it, thinking that when they stop liking it, they will quit this habit.

I once spoke to a lawyer and best-selling author, a man who stands before audiences hundreds strong, who eats his nails down to the flesh until there's no nail left, just fingers with pieces of skin. The surprising part is that he enjoys biting!

I'll share with you some of my personal experience: As someone who smoked for many years, I used to say that I smoke because I love smoking, and that I have no need to stop. So, what was it that did made me want to stop?

A year before I quit smoking, a relative, to whom I was very close, was diagnosed with cancer. When I came to visit him, I didn't smoke by his side. One time I came to visit with my then-eighteen month old son. The visit went on for a while and I was craving a cigarette. I asked my relative to watch over the boy, went down to have a smoke. When I came back to pick up my son, with the exquisite smell of cigarettes, I must have caused my relative a serious breathing irritation, because he started coughing terribly. I remember still being able to hear his coughs all the way to my car. At that moment I realized something important about myself - I was an addict!!! If I can't wait a few hours to smoke, and I have such a dire need for a cigarette, it just spells out, "Sarit, you are an addict, period!" Here is where I became aware of my addiction. I declared out loud to myself, "Sarit, you're an addict, get a hold of yourself and find a solution!" Thus began my journey to kick the habit. I know now how pathetic I was then with the cigarette and the countless excuses I've made for myself, such as that it didn't bother me or that I actually liked cigarettes.

The ex-biters that I've talked to said that they feel the same. After all, they don't really like seeing their nails bitten beyond recognition, but their need to bite has blinded them to the reality of their addiction. The excused it, like other addicts do with various habits, by saying they just like it.

The sentiment is true - we love the activity we perform, whether it's smoking, biting, eating, etc., it's just the consequences that we dislike. We're willing to ignore the result, as long as we don't have to give up the activity itself.

The idea is simple - calling a spade a spade: "I'm addicted to nail biting and I know that I can avoid biting, but I choose not to because I like biting!"

Do you really like being a nail biter? Do you really like seeing the blood around the nail? Do you really like walking with your hands in fists so people won't see the bites? Do you really like hearing comments from your peers and being asked why you bite? What is it that you really like? Just the act itself. Nail biting is considered a non-beneficial habit - one that doesn't assist us in resolving problems. It can be turned into another, more beneficial habit.

In previous chapters, several reasons were presented for why people bite, through which you can discover the true cause of your biting and simply change the habit. Most ex-smokers stop smoking and gain weight. Why? Because they replace one habit, smoking, with another, eating. They both have a similar root cause - a mental need to "fill the gap" which manifests itself in filling the oral cavity (if not with smoke then with food). They replace one non-beneficial habit with another non-beneficial habit.

I suggest that you replace the non-beneficial biting habit with a positive habit that can give you some silence, for example, a habit of breathing deeply, while concentrating on your breath; Deep breaths - three breaths and then five breaths. The point is to find an act more beneficial than biting your nails.

If you bite out of boredom, be aware of it: "I'm biting now because

I'm bored," and ask yourselves, "What can I do instead of biting? I'll find something that will benefit me and alleviate the boredom."

This way, every time something makes you bite, you'll ask "why am I biting?" and simply replace the nail biting with another habit - a more beneficial one.

In summation anyone can stop biting, even those who like it. First you must admit to yourself, that although you like the act, you can replace it with other, more beneficial activities. It's easy to see that you don't really like biting, but are addicted to it.

Exercises:
- **Find out the real reason that you like biting. What do you get out of it? Write about it in the attached pages.**

- **Write down three beneficial habits that can replace biting.**

- **Write down ten good things you like to do.**

- **Each time you intend to bite your nails, a second before you do, ask yourselves if you like yourselves at that moment.**

Now, after this exercise, you may now go back to biting!

Chapter 14

The Benefits of Nail Biting

This chapter comes right after the chapter about the biter who likes biting - its purpose is to see whether there are actual benefits to biting.

As previously stated, this book is suitable for those who really want to stop biting, and not for those who believe it's good for them or that just like the act. This chapter is for people who enjoy biting, since it will discusses its benefits in order to lift their spirits.

Are there Benefits to Nail Biting?

- You're a masochist creating sores and pains in your fingers, which become filled with puss due to biting the flesh.
- You like feeling shame and the need to hide your fingers in public.

- If you're a man, then you like concealing your fingers when you date a woman you like. If you're a woman, then you like concealing your fingers when you date a man you like.
- If you're a psychologist who speaks of changing habits and life situations, then you're a hypocrite because you do not change your own.
- If you like punishing yourself, and your biting habit is taken away, how will you be able to punish yourself?
- If you're a business executive, meeting with respectable people throughout your day, you are treated well despite your unaesthetic nails.
- Perhaps you think yourself a coward, who cannot face adversity without biting your nails or the skin around them.
- Or maybe you're just a cannibal who likes the taste of their own flesh. I recommend some seasoning before you bite…

This book is not for you, because you only see the benefits of biting!!!

In summation: In this chapter, we've seen how a biter only sees the benefits of biting and preserves them, so their habit that does them so much good isn't taken away.

I'm glad you've read this far. It's important to take all "benefits" into account and consider change.

Exercises:
- **Write down your perceived benefits of nail biting.**

- **Write down what biting gives you - the reason you preserve the habit.**

Chapter 15

The Main Causes of Fearing Decision

A decision, according to the dictionary definition, is a resolution, ruling, assertion, choice and judgment. All these word imply definitiveness, no going back.

When we think about decisions as something final, it can be a very intimidating, however relieving it may be. If I choose a certain path and decide, in our case, to stop biting my nails, there is no going back. Especially if the nail biting has granted me with relaxation and confidence - the very decision to stop will deny me of them.

Despite the perceived fatality of the idea, we always have the ability to change. The belief that a decision is fatal and final generates fear of making decisions. Thus, it's important to understand that the decision we make does not have to be final. Each choice and decision carries a price, but it does not have to be final, as opposed to irreversible decisions, such as the amputation of a limb.

My inspiration in writing this book comes from my own experience in quitting smoking. What drove me to chuck the cigarette (and the whole pack with it), is my decision "That's it - I quit!"

The decision was accompanied with heavy concerns: How will it turn out? How will I get by? What will I do when I'm bored? What will I do when I'm nervous? I really like smoking, how will I give it up? Many apprehensions, but that decision is what brought me success in quitting smoking. First make the decision - it gets easier from there.

The Main Reasons for Fear of Decisions

People are afraid of making decisions, because they entail responsibility and decisions come with a price. Making a decision or taking responsibility is not an easy thing. There is the option of not doing either and playing the victim: "I bite because my parents were biters," "It's genetic," "I can't quit," "I can't control it." All these statements free us from responsibility and make us a victim of external circumstance.

The second main reason is the fear of failure. We are afraid to fail, so we avoid making a decision. There's a clever riddle I heard once:

Five frogs are sitting on the dock. One decides to jump in the water. How many frogs remain on the dock?

The answer is five. Because the frog didn't jump; it just decided to jump.

Making a decision is not enough. We need to act upon it. Michael Jordan, the most well-known basketball player in history, once said: "I've missed more shots than I scored, and that is why I was the world's best player." If you don't shoot, you won't miss, but you'll also never score. If you let fear of failure paralyze you, you won't get results. In the case of nail biting, you'll continue complaining and living with dissatisfaction. You will never stop biting if you're paralyzed by fear.

The key to success in quitting nail biting is first and foremost making a decision!

Exercises:

- Make a list of two-three times when you struggled to make a decision and were happy you did in retrospect.

- Write down the worst of scariest thing that would happen to you if you made the decision to stop biting.

- After filling both lists, look at the first one - were there things you were afraid of and still overcame?

- After writing all that, write next to the articles in which you succeeded what helped you make the decision.

Chapter 16

What are the Alternatives for Biting?

In this chapter, we'll see if there are alternatives to nail biting and whether or not they're effective.

In various stores around the world, you'll find methods and patents to quit non-beneficial habits, such as nail biting. Is it practical to rely on a substitute, such as a French manicure, to stop someone from biting their nails?

Many years of experience have taught me that this is divided in two: There are those that benefit from artificial nails because they enjoy seeing a well-kept nail, and how much their hands are aesthetic and groomed. Then there are those that no matter how tidy and groomed their nails look - with red polish or with a white French that give the nail an amazing look - they go out smiling from ear to ear, and when I ask, "Well, will you take care of the nails this time? Look how much fun you have looking at them!" they smile and don't speak a word. Go out of my clinic and come back with a half-bitten hand, and sometimes with no nails at all.

When I ask them, "What happened not again? It was so beautiful and you were so happy when you left..." one looks at me with a smile and has nothing to say, another says, "I've had a rough week, don't ask..." and the third says: "Work was boring this week..." I hear a million other excuses. Some are certain that if I did their nails regularly even without a French manicure (because there isn't enough nail to build on), they'd be psyched that their natural nails are so pretty and groomed, that they would stop biting. So, they come in every week to treat the nails and apply polish so they can grow them out. In this case as well, some see a benefit from the French manicure for the long run, and some don't.

"I have over 40 nail polishes and nothing works." "I've tried a nibble inhibitor, different colors of polish... is there a solution to biting? I'm getting desperate..."

Can a French manicure or applying nail polish in various colors provide an alternative for biting?

There's also the nibble inhibitor. After profound research to understand how it works, I found out that there is some benefit from it. The taste is disgusting, so the biter can no longer put their finger in their mouth, which lets their nails grow unbitten.
Then there are those who apply it and are at first disgusted by the taste, but pretty soon they get accustomed to the taste and

go back to biting: "I put nibble inhibitor on my nails. It tasted disgusting at first, but I slowly got used to it, so it was bitter, but edible." So, can nibble inhibitor help?

There are all sorts of methods, such as hypnosis, dental accessories and others... some derive benefit from them and others don't.

Why don't these substitutes help everyone who tries them? Some people have a relatively mild addiction, in which case it can be cured by substitutes, while others who are more seriously addicted will not be satisfied with anything but the real thing, thus treating their symptoms is useless.

For the most part, the alternatives provide temporarily relief, and their users don't really acknowledge that they quit. For example, when I was pregnant with my older son, I stopped smoking. I also didn't smoke when I breastfed him. One day, when I wanted to return to work as an employee in my field, when the interviewer asked if I smoke, I said "Currently I'm not smoking because I'm nursing, but I am a smoker." After I stopped nursing, obviously I went back to smoking.

What happens with my clients who get French manicures and don't bite the artificial nail is that they tell me that they don't believe that the French has made them quit biting, only that it helps them keep their nails groomed, and that once they remove it they'll go back to biting them. Thus, quitting has to be internalized, stemming from a deep understanding of the need not to bite. If I truly want to stop biting, then I must replace my non-beneficial habit with a beneficial one.

I believe that the people who benefit from alternatives are those who need a slight push, a little willpower, which is why they managed to quit. I too, during the process of quitting smoking, applied willpower, chewed gum, which helped for a period of nine or ten months, after which I went back to smoking, until I discovered the method mentioned in the book.

The substitutes can assist in quitting a non-beneficial habit but only temporarily, if the addiction is severe. For example, if we take a person who smokes one or two cigarettes a day, they would have an easier time using a substitute and stop smoking compared to someone who smokes a pack or a pack and a half a day.
In this chapter, I'm emphasizing the heavy addicts, those who will not be satisfied with any substitute. It just won't do. Just as there are smoker who use an e-cigarette, plastic cigarette or nicotine patches as a substitute, there are those who manage to quit using alternative and those that don't.

I want to stress that to all of you who haven't succeeded in quitting nail biting that there is a possibility to stop biting, and that you can be one of those that make it. If you apply my method, you too can stop biting.

In summation: In this chapter, we've discussed the substitutes available in the market and whether they can help people quit biting, as well as who can benefit from them and why they don't always work.

Exercises:

- **Sit down for a few minutes with yourself and make a list of habits you've changed or quit throughout your life (if you believe that there isn't even one habit that you manage to change or quit, you can write down "I've started using the toilet instead of wearing diapers" or "stopped sucking on a pacifier" as a start. I believe that everyone has something that they've changed or quit.)**

- **Make a list of 5-10 possible replacements for biting, all sorts of habits which can benefit you instead of nail biting.**

Possible Substitutes for Biting

1.

2.

3.

4.

5.

6.

7.

8.

9.

10.

Chapter 17

Secret Addiction

Over the years caring for my clients' hands and feet, I've stumbled across an interesting phenomenon, there are those who bite the skin around the nail. French manicure has helped many of my clients stop biting their nails and they figured that they were over nail biting. But then I saw that they come in to me with sores around their nails, and realized that they just moved from the habit of nail biting to a habit of skin biting.

Skin biting stems from the reasons described in previous chapters. When one puts their finger in their mouths and starts messing with it in order to "even it out", the nail comes out completely chewed up. Sometimes, when biting the skin around the nail, the skin is pulled the wrong way and a painful sore is created, sometimes even an actual infection on the nail's side.

Evening out the nail is analogous to evening out a cake. You probably know this habit, after cutting a cake for your guests, it just won't do to leave the cut asymmetric, so you try to even it out, and that one isn't symmetric either so you even out some more and before you know it the cake is gone.

I've heard of this habit from many people who practice it regularly. This reminds me a lot of evening out the nail or arranging the skin around it. Those who "arrange" the skin are not aware of their addiction, to put something in their mouth, just as long as they don't have to discuss or understand what it is they want and need. Instead, they automatically put their hands in their mouths.

I asked a client of mine to pay attention as to why she feels the need to bite the nail and that each time she puts her hand in her mouth, examine why she does it. I told her, "There's no need for you to remove your hand from your mouth or that you stop biting. You just need to pay attention, so I can have more reasons and habits for the book I'm writing."

That same client came back after three weeks (nail fill is done once every two or three weeks), and told me that she was about to put her finger in every time she was upset and looked for a way to calm down, or when she got bored in class. Then she added - "But I didn't bite. I just put my hand in my mouth." She thought to herself, "That's it; I'm through biting, yay me." At first I only listened to her, before looking at her hand's condition. When I started treatment, I saw that she did stop biting her nails, but her hand was filled with sores around her nail. I asked her, "And what's this?" and she said, "Oh, that' nothing - I had some skin on the side that bugged me and I had to get rid of it."

This is a hidden addiction - the thought that the biting has stopped, while simultaneously biting the skin around the nail. It's just a cosmetic change, no pun intended.

When I stopped smoking cigarettes, I opened the fridge door more often and started gaining weight. I came to my senses and asked myself, "What are you doing, you've traded one bad habit for another." I tried to be more aware of what I'm putting in my mouth and checked every time I opened the fridge - "Am I hungry? Or is my appetite mental or emotional?" This way, I've curbed my fridge door habit as well, since I realized I was trading one addiction for another.

Food or cigarette won't really help me relax, focus or avoid boredom. It just won't do me any good. Every time I wanted to pop a cigarette, even after quitting, I'd asked myself, "Sarit, does this benefit you? Would it get you anywhere?" And then I'd search my soul to find what would help me. Many times, I found out that I don't really need it. As fast as the urge came, it was gone. The more time passes; the craving comes and goes faster, so that sometimes it passes so quickly that I don't even have to bother with the questions.

Skin biting, or "evening out" the skin around the nail, as my clients say, is the same exact addiction as nail biting.

I've also heard of people evening out toenails. It's the same idea as it is with fingernails. I've heard of people who tear off toenails to the point of bleeding, just like with the skin around the fingernail. This behavior is rooted in the same reasons and habits and it's the same addiction, except you don't put anything in your mouth. Later on, you'll read about the solution to this entire addiction but until then, I do not ask you to stop biting, or to stop "adjusting" the skin around the nail or to stop tearing toenails, but just to pay attention while you're doing it.

Exercises:
- **Look at the skin you want to chew because it bugs you, and ask one question: Is it really an aesthetic desire or do you just want to bite?**

- **Buy a small nail clipper that you can keep in your bag or your car; it will help you later on to stop biting your skin.**

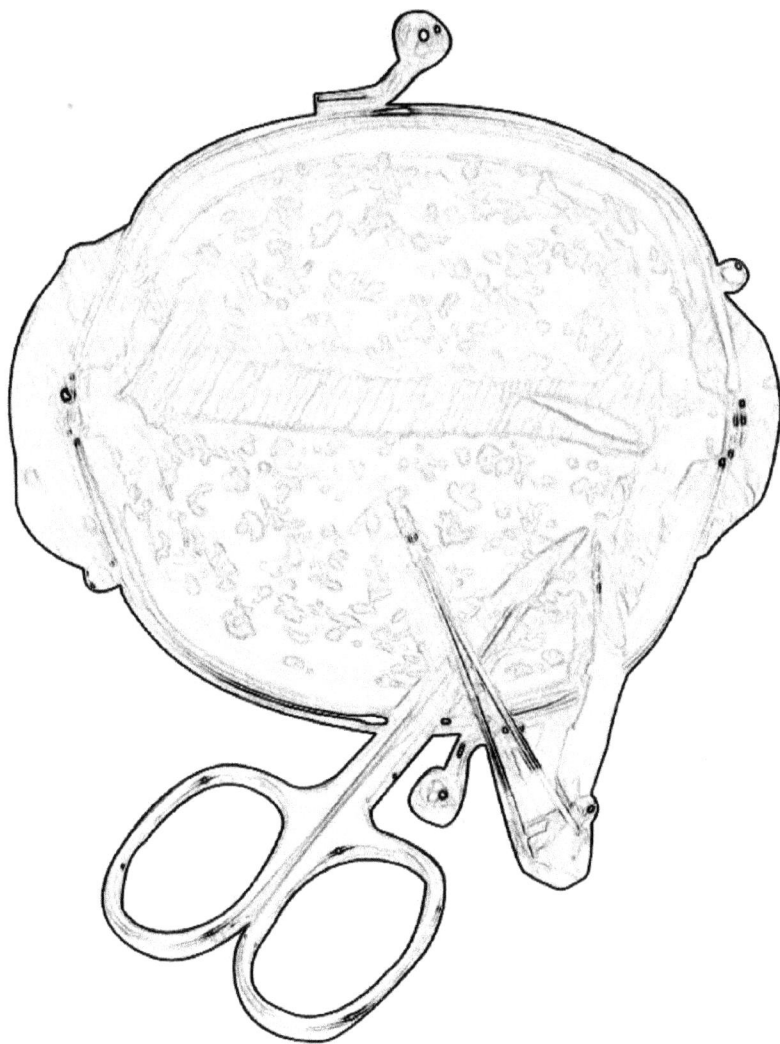

Things to Think About:

Chapter 18

Two Reasons Why Quitting Can Fail

Many times in life we see that there are no conclusive results, and since every individual is different, with a different life experience, not everyone can succeed in quitting right away. There are several reasons why quitting nail biting can fail or be difficult:

The first is the availability of the nails - they're always with you. Contrary to cigarettes, which you can stop buying when you decide to quit smoking, nails are with us everywhere. So, it's important that you remember that there's no such thing as "just one nail," or "just evening it out," or "just the edge of the skin around the nail," because that is the trap you trigger: Soon enough you'll want to "take care" of another nail and then another.

The second reason is a bad day. Always remember than even before you stopped biting, you've had good days and bad days. Life has its ups and downs, just like a hospital patient monitor: When the patient is alive, the line moves up and down alternately, and when he's dead it becomes a flat line. I'm sure you'd rather have your monitor displaying the former. I remind you that if you've stopped biting through your own willpower, you'd give in long ago. If the choice is between losing and not gaining, why would we want to lose? I remember that each time I said, "I'm going on a diet," I immediately became hungry. It's amazing how the moment you force yourself to give something up, we just crave it more. So, if we have a bad day and choose to see ourselves as victims and are overcome by the thought "I'm giving into nail biting" - the bad day becomes a lot worse, since our guilt is added on top of our giving up.

If you're having a bad day, it's important that you remind yourselves that sometimes there are days like that and it could be worse, regardless of quitting nail biting. Remember that it's like rough seas: Even when the tide is high, the waves reach the shore and calm down.

Instead of getting tense or depressed, take a deep breath and remind yourselves that going back to biting won't help you turn the bad day into a good one. Promise yourselves that tomorrow will be much better and look for something positive within you, like "It's so great that I'm not a nail biter anymore!" and pat yourself on the back. When I'm in an off mood, I look at the things I have to be thankful for in my life - three to five thanks, and I regain my perspective. Sometimes I am thankful for the beautiful weather, for my two wonderful boys or for my amazing clients who keep coming back to me after so many years. Every time, I find something new to be thankful for and it changes from time to time.

I was a heavy smoker, and once I freed myself of that dependence, it was the greatest gift I could get. Even during tough times like my divorce, when I crave a cigarette, I'd take a deep breath and ask myself, "Well Sarit, say you light a cigarette now and have a smoke - would that make things right? Is that fraction of a second worth throwing it all away to have a smoke?" and less than a minute later, the need to smoke was gone entirely. This would repeat every few months and today, after six years without smoking, those moments don't happen anymore. Once you become free of the nail biting dependence, you realize how useless it was in the   first place. That's the lesson I learned, as did other clients of mine who stopped biting.

The idea is to understand that your bad days have nothing to do with the question of whether you're biting or not. I say the same to those who bite out of a need to focus or alleviate boredom: Remind yourselves that in times of crisis, you don't need to bite your skin or nails. Neither will make you more focused or less bored.

In summation, there are two scenarios that can make you fall off the wagon and go back to biting: The first is the thought that since your nails are available 24/7 it'd be okay to bite just one. I remind you that it's just like that sip of wine for a recovering alcoholic. One hit and they'll go for the whole bottle. It's the same with you - one "evening out" or "adjustment" of the mail, or even a touch at the edge of the skin around the nail, and you go right back to biting. Mark my words!

The second scenario is the bad day. So take a deep breath, remind yourselves how wonderful you are and what you have to be thankful for in life. Recall your successes. It will help you make that switch. Most of all, remember that no matter how many nails you bite, it won't make your day better. So wouldn't it be a shame to take a step backward?

Exercises:
- **Make a list of 30 good things in your life that you're thankful for.**

- **Read five of them every day, and start over when you reach the end.**

- **Practice breathing - every night, before turning in, count your breaths. Look outward and count as you inhale.**

Chapter 19

Kicking It

This is the chapter readers usually look for even before reading the book, since its human nature to look for shortcuts, and the whole purpose of the book is quitting, so why not skip straight to here?

Sorry to disappoint you! If you truly want to kick your nail biting habit, you'll find that this chapter is not an abbreviated solution. To kick any habit, you have to undergo a process.

Below is a detailed process of quitting in four stages. It would be a bad idea to skip any of the stages. Instead, you should meticulously progress from one stage to the next until the process is complete.

Stage One: The Will to decide
The most crucial part of the process is to make the decision to stop biting! The will must come from within you. If you want to quit nail biting, you must focus and use your willpower. It is only through willpower that we don't relent from the idea of stopping the habit to bite and focus on the idea of withdrawal from nail biting despite the many temptations.

Stage Two: Elevating awareness
Once you start thinking why you do a certain act (and cancel your

conscious autopilot), your level of awareness rises. You begin to understand that certain acts, such as nail biting, stem from other needs rather than the evident ones.

We all have the ability to achieve everything we set our minds to, as long as we expand our level of awareness adequately. All we have in life is a direct expression of our level of awareness.

If we want to change non-beneficial habits, we must refer to them consciously in order to elevate our level of awareness.

The change in your awareness is occurring in this very moment, while you're reading this book. You'll have a new understanding of the way you behave and the way in which you'll stop nail biting.

For example, my level of awareness as a parent increases more and more, and thanks to it I become a more attentive mother, a better mother. Had my level of awareness to parenting been low, I believe that I'd have more difficulty compared to my experience of parenting today. The more I endeavor to elevate my awareness, through forethought and questions such as "Why am I doing this?", "Why am I getting upset?" or "What's really bothering me?" my level of frustration and anger toward the kids diminishes.

Another example: If a person wants to invest in the stock market based on blind luck, their chances of profiting is lower than that of a person who studied the field and elevated their level of awareness to know the right time to invest and what to invest in, so that his future profits will increase.

It is necessary to understand why we bite, what biting does for us or what brought us to a situation in which we need or want to bite. It is important to read the entire book in the written order. The chapter structure and the exercises given after each chapter are crucial. Writing down the answers will elevate your awareness of yourself.

Stage Three: Make the Decision

This is a very important step in the withdrawal process. After you read the entire book and perform all exercises, comes the critical part - the decision stage!!

Anything we want to achieve in life must be accompanied by a decision.

Even on a day-to-day basis, we make a lot of decisions: For example, choosing what we want to eat or drink in the morning. First we make a choice, and then we carry it out.

The stage in which we think that "Today is the best day for me to quit biting!" is crucial. Moreover, the choice of day is also important, since we wouldn't want to start the withdrawal process before a major or stressful event. The decision should be made during a pleasant, relaxed period.

Stage Four: Stick With It

Any withdrawal from a habit, whatever it may be - smoking or alcohol, pacifier or diapers - takes at least three consecutive weeks. The process of withdrawal takes about 21 consecutive days during which any pause, even for one day, restarts the count.

When deciding to stop nail biting, you should know that there will be hard times following the decision, but remember that after 21 consecutive days you'll experience enlightenment; something will click. This feeling will have you asking yourself, "Why was I even biting? I didn't even need it!"

I had a hard time when I began my withdrawal of smoking, since when quitting cigarettes, the body needs to release its nicotine addiction, i.e. it's not just a mental withdrawal. I knew I had to wait five days until the body will no longer need nicotine. I knew that the fifth day was the hardest, but remembered that it takes five days for physical withdrawal, and tried my hardest to restrain myself. I said to myself, let's see how I feel after five days, what do I have to lose? After that, there were 21 more days of withdrawal, and every time I felt a need to smoke, I thought about why I need a cigarette. I imagined the cigarette in my mouth, and the need just vanished. I'll give an example: On a day when I was anxious and would normally use a cigarette to calm down (but I can't, since I decided I won't smoke anymore and needed to go through withdrawal), I said to myself: "Well, Sarit, imagine that you have a cigarette in your mouth and your anxiousness goes away. It's true that the cigarette, like nail biting, doesn't make it go away, but let's pretend that it does." So I imagined the cigarette in my mouth. I could really feel myself taking a drag, and I couldn't believe how after a few seconds - not minutes, but seconds - the need for a cigarette was gone, and I was dedicated to the solution of the problem which led to the anxiousness, instead of ignoring it like a did for years.

You can do the same. Each time you want to bite, imagine the finger going in your mouth. You're probably saying to yourself, "Sure, cigarettes won't always be available so there are times when you can just imagine them. But our fingers are always there." Well, I have news for you: Today, there are cigarettes in every convenience store, grocery store and supermarket, even sold as singles so you don't have to buy a whole pack. In an age when every teenager can get their hands on cigarettes, they become very available.

After making the decision to stop biting, you'll find that your nails are available, but you wouldn't want to put them in your mouth, at least not during the trial period. I believe that you'd want to give yourself an opportunity not to bite for 21 full days. After all, what have you got to lose? You can always go back to biting. Just give yourself 21 consecutive days.

I assure you that after those 21 days, you'd feel the change. You'll look and feel better and actually have no desire to put your finger in your mouth. You grow out nice and pretty, and you'll feel that it would be a shame to ruin it. But I must warn the ladies among you - after the nails turn pretty, you'll want to groom them with a nice polish or pattern…
I'll share with you a story about one of my clients, a senior clinical psychologist. When I met her for the first time, I was just taking my first steps in my line of work, and she told me that she wanted a manicure, but can't have one because she bites her nails. I stared at her with bewilderment - I couldn't believe that a clinical psychologist, who's supposed to take care of people, could bite her nails. I didn't mention it to her; I just asked her if she still wanted me to see if there was anything I can do for

her. She was skeptic, but agreed to entrust me with her fingers and what was left of her nails. Fortunately, she hadn't bitten them all the way through, just to the white part of the nail so I still had something to work with. I filed the remaining nails, applied base polish and then drew a flower pattern on each and every nail. She couldn't believe how pretty her hand looked, and decided that she would care for them from now on. Every week or two she would set an appointment, and after several weeks she stopped coming in. She told me that she kicked the habit, which brought me much joy.

After a few months, I heard from her again. "Sarit, you have to help me again. I went back to biting and I want to set an appointment for a manicure and nail polish while I still have fingernails left." I treated her and drew her favorite pattern, flowers, and so every week or two we'd have a session.

Today, after several years of grooming her nails, she has natural nails that she's proud of.

I've told you this story, but I also have to warn you that even if you've quit and don't bite anymore, you'll always be tempted and think that "If I've quit once, I can do it again," or "Okay, it's just one nail." Well, don't. It's important to remember that you'll always be nail biters, even if you quit. The craving always returns.
Think of an alcoholic who quit drinking and is not allowed even a sip of sacramental wine, because it would remind them of the enjoyment they had from drinking, the relaxing sensation, which silenced their pain and their inner dialogue. They might forget the excruciating withdrawal period or why they even wanted to quit. I can tell you that after a few years without smoking, in a rough

period like a divorce, I really wanted to smoke and told myself, "Just one smoke." But then I remembered that I was just like an alcoholic and that I mustn't. I took a few deep breaths and occupied myself until the need was gone.

One other important matter is habit replacement. It's very important to know that when you stop biting, you must find another, harmless habit for the duration of the withdrawal. I assure you, you'll only need the substitute for a short period, and perhaps during crisis periods. When quitting smoking, one could gain weight. It happens because they haven't found another habit, and when the mouth is not busy with a cigarette, it's busy with food. I too was one of the gainers - 8 kilo - but very soon I balanced myself and lost them, so it is possible to stop biting without side effects and you can do it too!!

Six years have passed since I stopped smoking. On the fifth year, I the urge to smoke completely, as if I never smoked. Before quitting, I could smoke two packs a day, so I know for certain that nail biting can be quit just like smoking can be. The most crucial part is sticking to the method and of course, truly wanting it.

In summation: Quitting nail biting entails four stages:

First - Will
Second - Increasing awareness
Third - Making the decision
Fourth - 21 days of withdrawal
Review all four stages, and I guarantee that you succeed in quitting nail biting.

Things to Think About:

Chapter 20

Being Tempted to Bite Again

In this chapter, we'll highlight coping with the temptation to bite again, and how to avoid tempting situations.

Before making the decision - Now I stop biting - there is that fear: How will I do without it? I suggested to a client during treatment: "Make a commitment now that you won't bite until the next treatment." Of course, at the time she hadn't read the book and did not know my method. She looked at me with startled eyes. I told her: "It's only for two weeks (usually with clients who bite the artificial nails last for three weeks, sometimes more. I schedule their appointments every two weeks instead of three). She answered, "I decide not to decide." She was very insistent on not making the decision.

In this chapter, we'll highlight coping with the temptation to bite again, and how to avoid tempting situations.

Before making the decision - Now I stop biting - there is that fear: How will I do without it? I suggested to a client during treatment: "Make a commitment now that you won't bite until the next treatment." Of course, at the time she hadn't read the book and did not know my method. She looked at me with startled eyes. I told her: "It's only for two weeks (usually with clients who bite the artificial nails last for three weeks, sometimes more. I schedule their appointments every two weeks instead of three). She answered, "I decide not to decide." She was very insistent on not making the decision.

Today, after two weeks of coming to me for treatment, she is over nail biting, and now comes in one every three to three and a half weeks.

The major concern of every former biting addict, and certainly of every ex-smoker, is: "How will I do without it." This fear doesn't stem from withdrawal symptoms - it is an emotional fear of life without biting, fear of the unknown. Like everything in life, we don't know what to expect, emotionally and physically. We are paralyzed by fear. One must understand that fear is equal to expectation of pain. It's basically a new idea which enters the conscious part of our mind. This new idea wants to replace an old one which doesn't want to be replaced.

I remember that when I started my withdrawal from smoking, before I realized how easy it was for me to stop smoking, I would use my willpower (which is very strong when I need it), and made a decision to stop smoking. I remember smoking cigarettes hastily and stressfully. The conscious decision that I'm about to stop smoking made me panic and become terribly stressed. Similarly, every time I decided to go on a diet - I suddenly got hungrier, and instead of cutting down, I found myself eating more than usual.

Fear of the unknown exists every time we want to make a change toward something unfamiliar. When I was a child, my parents sent me to learn swimming at Tel Aviv University, where most of the professional athletes train with one of the best teachers available. Allegedly, I already knew how to swim, but I refused to take my floats off. My parents were baffled. One day, we drove to Kinneret Lake's western coast, where the waves were very high during the evenings. Then all of a sudden, with no apparent reason, I agreed to take the floats off. I said, "Dad! Mom! I want to go in the water without floats." They were worried about me because the waves were high, but they let me anyway, and I've been swimming without them ever since. There's a reason they say "Jump into the deep end."

That fear, of stopping nail biting, is merely an emotional fear. It's a fear that you're dependent on something and you can't do without it. Believe in yourself, and throw yourself into the water. Once you've thrown yourself in, you'll find out that this fear is pointless and that you can deal with every difficult situation without biting your nails.

One must understand that the temptation is great, since your fingernails will always be there. If you say to yourself that you're only trying to stop biting and that you'll always have your nails in a decision to stop smoking. I remember smoking cigarettes hastily and stressfully. The conscious decision that I'm about to stop smoking made me panic and become terribly stressed. Similarly, every time I decided to go on a diet - I suddenly got hungrier, and instead of cutting down, I found myself eating more than usual.

Fear of the unknown exists every time we want to make a change toward something unfamiliar. When I was a child, my parents sent me to learn swimming at Tel Aviv University, where most of the professional athletes train with one of the best teachers available. Allegedly, I already knew how to swim, but I refused to take my floats off. My parents were baffled. One day, we drove to Kinneret Lake's western coast, where the waves were very high during the evenings. Then all of a sudden, with no apparent reason, I agreed to take the floats off. I said, "Dad! Mom! I want to go in the water without floats." They were worried about me because the waves were high, but they let me anyway, and I've been swimming without them ever since. There's a reason they say "Jump into the deep end."

That fear, of stopping nail biting, is merely an emotional fear. It's a fear that you're dependent on something and you can't do without it. Believe in yourself, and throw yourself into the water. Once you've thrown yourself in, you'll find out that this fear is pointless and that you can deal with every difficult situation without biting your nails.

One must understand that the temptation is great, since your fingernails will always be there. If you say to yourself that you're only trying to stop biting and that you'll always have your nails in case of emergency, you will fail. Once you understand that you have control, you'll be able to say to yourself, "It's so great that I'm not biting anymore!" Then, even if you get stressed out or have a bad day, you won't have to turn to that habit that you've kicked, i.e. nail biting - you'll understand and know well that it'll get you nowhere. No matter how strong the temptation is, remind yourself that "It's so great that I'm not biting anymore!" You control the habit, and not the other way around!

In summation, you are in control. You'll see that the fear of making a decision whether to continue biting or stopping is purely emotional, fear of the unknown. I assure you that when you're past the decision making process, you won't bite anymore. In any tempting situation you'll face - obviously I wouldn't recommend testing yourself intentionally in stressful situations - you'll know that biting will not benefit you or solve the difficult situation for you, and the temptation to bite will disappear completely. You'll always be able to go back and read through the book if you feel weak or unconfident. You haven't stopped biting through sheer willpower, but through awareness of what you'll gain by not biting.

Exercises:

- Make a list of every action you were denied from by the unknown on which you gave up.

- Make a list of things you were afraid of doing and acted despite fear, and what you felt like after doing them.

Chapter 21

Summary

This book can help every nail biter - women, men, teens and children - if they want to change this habit. I wrote this book to inspire those who believe quitting is impossible. I could have named the book "How to Quit any Bad Habit" and not focus on nail biting, since this book contains many exercises which can be implemented for every addiction. I chose to focus on an area which I encounter every day, which is nail biting. It's an area with which I've been closely familiar for many years, and it's important for me to help those who want to help themselves.

You've read chapter after chapter and completed the exercises, and without noticing, you've slowly begun to kick non-beneficial habits, keep better looking fingers and be more aware of yourself.

We've undergone a profound journey into our minds to try to understand how nail biting benefits us and how it doesn't. I've shared with you many of my experiences I had throughout years of treating my clients, and the experiences of people who've been interviewed for the book.

All of our habits are our own doing, whether consciously or not. This is also the reason that we can reshape them every time. This book has also shown us that our habits, the ones which drive us and the unwanted ones.

In reading this book, we've learned a complete process of shaping and creating new habits.

After identifying the habits as non-beneficial and wanting to change them, we've seen how one can assimilate new habits in their place. The reason for finding new habits is that if we don't consciously choose a new, beneficial habit, there is a high probability that the new habit will generate the same dependency and the same addiction caused by nail biting.

We've understood that there are barriers within us, and that in order to stop we must take significant action, because it's all up to us. When you stop nail biting, you must quickly pick up a new, beneficial habit.

I wish you great success, and I believe that if one person made it, anyone can, through perseverance. As long as we pay attention to ourselves, it'll be smooth sailing, without struggling or going to extremes.

Through this book, you'll be able to rid yourself of the fears that manage your life. You have the power; you're the captain on deck! Good luck!

This book was published thanks to a group of remarkable people who helped me, supported me, and who filled me with inspiration. They made suggestions, pushed forward, commented and enlightened. Thanks to these people the book was published. Thank you all!!!

I'd like to thank Amir Harduf, CEO of Harduf Business Coaching, and Israel's leading consultant for marketing success in small businesses. Attorney Yaniv Zeid, CEO of "The Art of Persuasion" and a popular business novelist. They were my mentors in writing this book who helped me focus my knowledge and put it on paper. Personal thanks to Attorney Yaniv Zeid, who personally coached me and inspired me on what to write and what to focus on.

A big thanks to Yossi Friedlander, who helped me overcome my fears and put my knowledge on paper, and accompanied all throughout writing the book.

Big thanks to Doron Moshe for the push I needed to make this book a reality!

Thanks to my two boys, Niv and Noam, who were part of the process.
Thanks to my amazing clients and friends, who greatly inspired me, and agreed that I share their stories as examples in the book. Thanks for the support and endless encouragement.

And now it's your turn…

Dear readers, I've gathered the required experience from quitting smoking and from my clients' endeavors with quitting nail biting, and have turned them into a book intended for those who wish to stop biting.

Your life experience and the process you've undergone in this book are very important to me and could be used in future publications.

I would love to read your experience and of course, answer every question of issue you may have.

Phone: 054-495-8685

Email: sasherov@gmail.com

Facebook: www.facebook.com/saritasherov

Website: www.asarit.co.il

Yours,
Sarit Asherov
Rosenzwei

www.ingramcontent.com/pod-product-compliance
Lightning Source LLC
Chambersburg PA
CBHW061827040426
42447CB00012B/2856